The Spider

Gunilla Ingves

A & C Black · London

A & C Black (Publishers) Ltd, 35 Bedford Row,
London WC1R 4JH
First published by Natur och Kultur, Sweden under the series title *Har du sett på...*

Translated by Jane Sutton
Nature advisor English text, Jean Imrie

Ingves, Gunilla
Spider. – (First nature books)
1. The Spider – Juvenile literature
I. Title II. Spindeln. *English*
III. Series
595.4'4 QL458.4
ISBN 0-7136-2650-X

ISBN 0-7136-2650-X

This edition arranged with the help of Angus Hudson, London
Printed and bound in Great Britain by Purnell and Son (Book Production) Ltd., Paulton, Bristol

It is a lovely day in spring. In the garden, a male spider is following some threads he has found on the ground.

The threads were made by a female spider. Here she is, next to her hole. The male spider is waiting in the grass.

The female spider goes over to the male spider, and they mate. Before long, there will be lots of young spiders.

After they have mated, the male quickly runs away. The female spider is much bigger than the male spider. She might think he is food and want to eat him.

Ten days later, the female spider is ready to lay her eggs. First she spins a carpet with her threads. Then she spins a light blue cocoon to lay her eggs in.

When the cocoon is full of eggs, the spider closes it up. She ties the cocoon to her body with some more threads.

Just in time, the spider hides in her hole. She sees a blackbird's yellow beak snap shut above the hole. She is safe in her hole and has a rest.

But the spider can't rest for long. She has to find food. Here is a nice fly to eat. She quietly creeps up behind the fly.

Then she pounces on the fly. But her cocoon falls off.
The spider hurries to tie it back on. The fly escapes.

After two weeks, the cocoon splits and out come lots of young spiders. They all crawl on the mother spider's back. The mother spider can get rid of the cocoon now.

The mother spider is hiding with her young spiders in a clump of grass. Along comes a flea beetle.

The mother spider runs up behind the flea beetle. Some of the young spiders fall off. The mother spider pounces on the flea beetle and sinks her poison fangs into it. The poison stuns the flea beetle so that it can't move.

The spider sucks all the juice from the beetle. Only the beetle's shell is left. The young spiders have time to catch up with their mother. They are not allowed to eat the beetle. They don't need food yet.

After a few weeks, the young spiders are ready to leave their mother. One morning, each young spider climbs to the top of a blade of grass. The spiders lift their backs and begin to spin some threads.

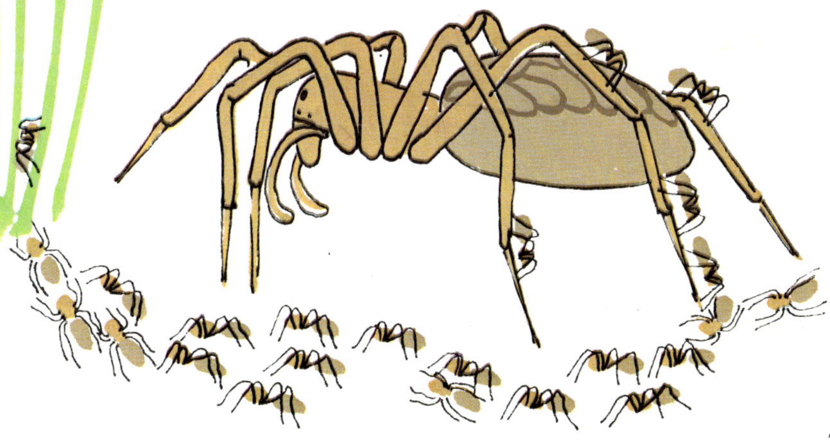

The threads are so light that they float upwards in the warm morning air. The young spiders let go of the blades of grass and float off like balloons.

One of the spiders floats a long way off. It lands on a leaf. A little girl sees it and picks the leaf.

The little girl looks very closely at the spider. The spider has eight eyes.

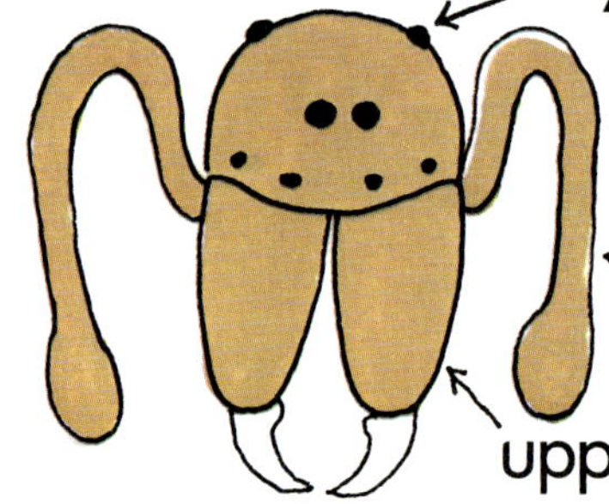

The spider's mouth has two upper jaws, like a pair of scissors. On each jaw there is a poison fang. The spider also has two palps. It uses its palps to hold things.

On the front part of its body, the little spider has eight legs. At the back of its body are six spinnerets. The spider spins its thread with these.

Now the spider wants to get off the leaf. It spins a thread and sticks it to the edge of the leaf. Then it spins some more thread to lower itself to the ground.

The spider hurries away to a stone and hides. It is very hungry. Here comes a tiny fly. The spider finds lots of other little insects to eat.

As the spider grows bigger, its skin gets too tight. One day, the skin splits open. The spider has a new skin underneath. This happens lots of times as the spider grows.

Now the spider is fully grown. It has to make itself a home. It digs a hole in the earth.

The spider uses its jaws to
dig and carries away the
earth with its palps.

Now the spider has finished making its hole. It sees a garden spider which is busy spinning its web in a nearby bush. The garden spider cannot see very well, so it has to catch insects in its web.

When the spider has finished looking at the garden spider's web, it dashes away to hunt for food.

Spring

David Lambert

Wayland

Titles in this series

Spring
Summer
Autumn
Winter

Edited by Andrew Kelly
Designed by Malcolm Smythe

First published in 1986 by
Wayland (Publishers) Ltd
61 Western Road, Hove
East Sussex BN3 1JD, England

British Library Cataloguing in Publication Data
Lambert, David, 1932 –
Spring.—(The Seasons)
1. Spring—Juvenile literature
I. Title II. Series
574.5'43 QH81

HARDBACK ISBN 0–85078–839–0

PAPERBACK ISBN 0–7502–0562–8

Typeset by Alphabet Limited, London.
Printed and bound by Casterman S.A., Belgium.

Contents

What seasons are

The times of year we call the seasons are natural periods marked by changes in the weather and differing lengths of day and night. In the temperate regions of the world there are four seasons: spring, summer, autumn and winter.

The word 'season' comes from an old Latin word for 'sowing'. Sowing, ploughing, and many more farm and garden activities are timed to fit in with the seasons.

Spring is the time when many flowers come out in gardens, parks and in the countryside.

'Spring' comes from an Anglo-Saxon word for 'rising'. In spring the sun rises higher in the sky each day and the days quickly lengthen. Spring is traditionally the time when the fields are ploughed and the crops are planted. Birds which left for warmer places the previous autumn return to mate and to build nests. Flowers burst forth and many young animals both on farms and in the countryside are born in spring. After the long sleep of the cold winter the earth awakens and life begins anew.

Seasons are not the same everywhere. In the northern and southern halves of the world the seasons are reversed as this chart shows:

	Northern Hemisphere		
Spring	*Summer*	*Autumn*	*Winter*
March April May	June July August	September October November	December January February
Autumn	*Winter*	*Spring*	*Summer*
	Southern Hemisphere		

Even in the same half of the world seasons differ from place to place. Much of Africa, southern Asia, South America, and Australia are always warm. There are no cold winters there like those of Canada or Britain. Many hot lands have just two seasons: wet and dry. Cold countries of the far north and far south have only two seasons: dark and light.

Many young animals are born in spring as there is plenty of food available for them to eat and it is not too cold.

Why seasons happen

The earth spins on its axis, an imaginary line drawn through the centre of the earth from the North Pole to the South Pole, once every twenty-four hours. This gives us day and night.

As well as turning on its axis, the earth orbits the sun once a year. The earth's axis is not vertical but tilted and it is this tilt which gives us the changing seasons as the earth orbits the sun.

During winter the Northern Hemisphere is facing away from the sun, and so the sun is lower in the sky in winter than in summer. Because the sun is lower in the sky in winter the rays of sunlight are more spread out when they strike the ground and the sun spends less time above the horizon which makes the days shorter. Also in winter the sun's rays must pass through more atmosphere, so they lose more energy. Weak, spread out rays of sunlight and short days mean that winter is colder than summer.

Each season starts when the sun is overhead at some special place.

Northern spring and southern autumn start about 21 March. Now the sun is overhead at the equator, an imaginary line around the middle of the earth. Day and night are the same length everywhere. This is called an equinox.

Day and night

Every twenty-four hours the earth completes one turn about its axis. This rotation causes day and night.

Polar and tropical sunlight

As you move away from the tropics towards either Pole the same amount of sunlight covers a larger and larger area due to the curvature of the earth. The sunlight therefore becomes less concentrated as you move towards either Pole and the climate becomes cooler. This diagram shows the earth at one of the equinoxes.

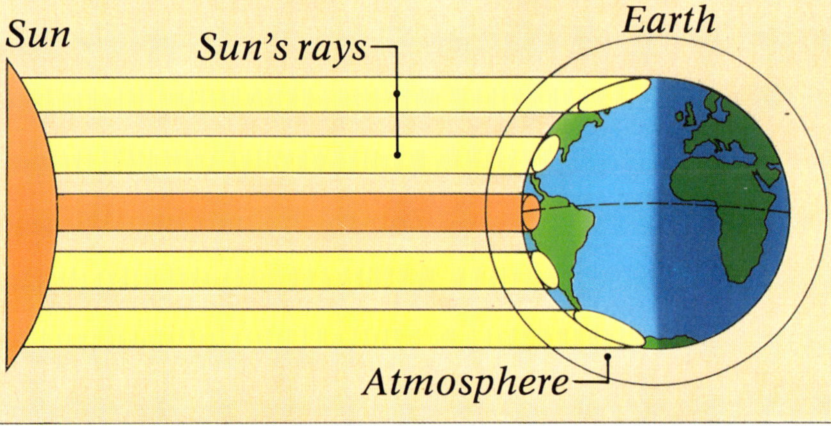

This photograph of earth, taken from space, shows night following day as the earth rotates.

Northern summer and southern winter start about 21 June. The position of the sun has moved as far north as it will go. Now is the Northern Hemisphere's longest day and shortest night and the Southern Hemisphere's shortest day and longest night. This is one of the solstices.

Southern spring and northern autumn start about 23 September. The sun is back above the equator and day and night are equal everywhere again.

Northern winter and southern summer start about 21 December. Now the position of the sun is as far to the south as it will go.

This diagram shows how the tilt of the earth means that the amount of light and heat reaching different parts of the earth varies through the year with the changing seasons.

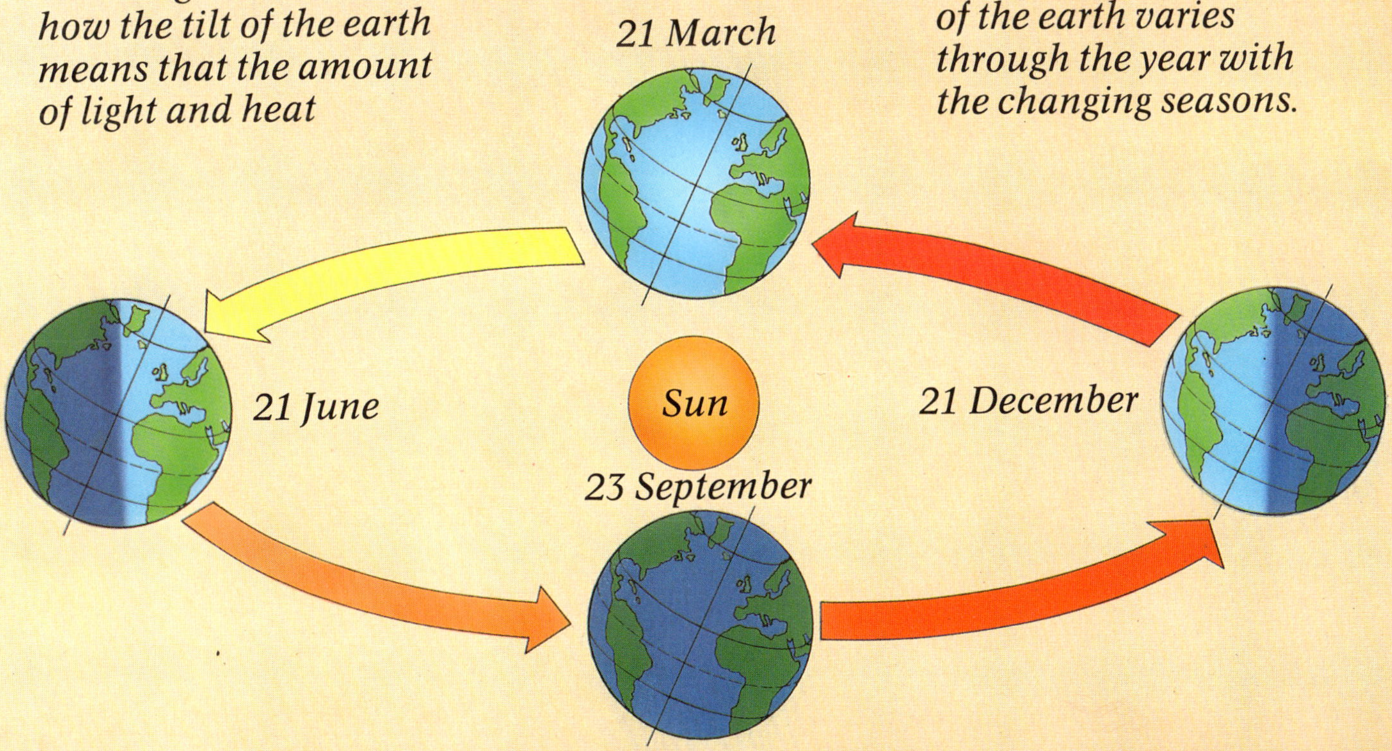

Spring weather

Everyone looks forward to spring. The days are longer and the sun rises higher in the sky each day. The weather grows warmer. This is the season when winter changes into summer, but winter weather often reappears and spring can be the wettest season of the year. Weather at this time of the year can be unsettled and even violent. The sun melts the snow and ice that has built up over winter and sometimes there can be floods. It is because the sun has to melt this snow and ice, and dry wet ground before it warms the air that spring is usually colder than autumn.

In some tropical regions, it is the time when the summer monsoonal rains arrive. When the first rain starts to fall it is a time for great celebration in places like India where the crops depend on these rains.

Avalanches, vast snow slides, are commonest in spring as warm rains or winds loosen the foundations of large masses of snow and ice that have formed over winter. Avalanches can be very destructive. In the European Alps whole villages have been swept away.

In some areas there are strong local winds. The sirocco is a hot, dry and

Some spring days are noted for their magnificent weather.

There are many avalanches in spring as warm wind or rain melts the snow.

sometimes dusty wind that blows out of the Sahara Desert and across the Mediterranean where it picks up moisture from the sea, becoming very humid by the time it reaches Italy. Similar hot, dry winds blow out of the interior of Australia in a southerly direction and are called brickfielders. On the great plains of the USA and USSR, narrow whirling funnels of air called tornadoes, the world's fiercest winds, can pluck up trees and houses and overturn cars. Tornadoes can occur at any time of the year but are five times more common in spring and summer.

Tornadoes occur most often in spring and summer.

Springtime around the world

Spring is very different in different parts of the world. To some lands it comes early and to others late or not at all. The world is always hot near the equator and always cold near the poles. Spring and autumn are seasons of the middle latitudes where it is neither very hot nor very cold.

Spring in the temperate regions is the time when days grow longer and warmer. Where there is snow, it melts. The plants and animals respond to the warmth. Flowers appear above the ground and animals that have slept through the winter wake up. Most animals become more active in spring. Migrant birds arrive and begin to build nests. Many insect eggs hatch. Bees begin collecting pollen again. Moths and butterflies that have spent the winter as chrysalises emerge and dry their wings in the sun.

In many parts of the temperate regions, spring is the time when fields

The earth can be divided into a number of different climatic zones. Each zone has different sorts of seasons. The temperate zone has spring, summer, winter and autumn. The polar zones have a long dark winter and a short cool summer. The tropics have hot wet and cooler, dry periods although some parts are always hot and wet.

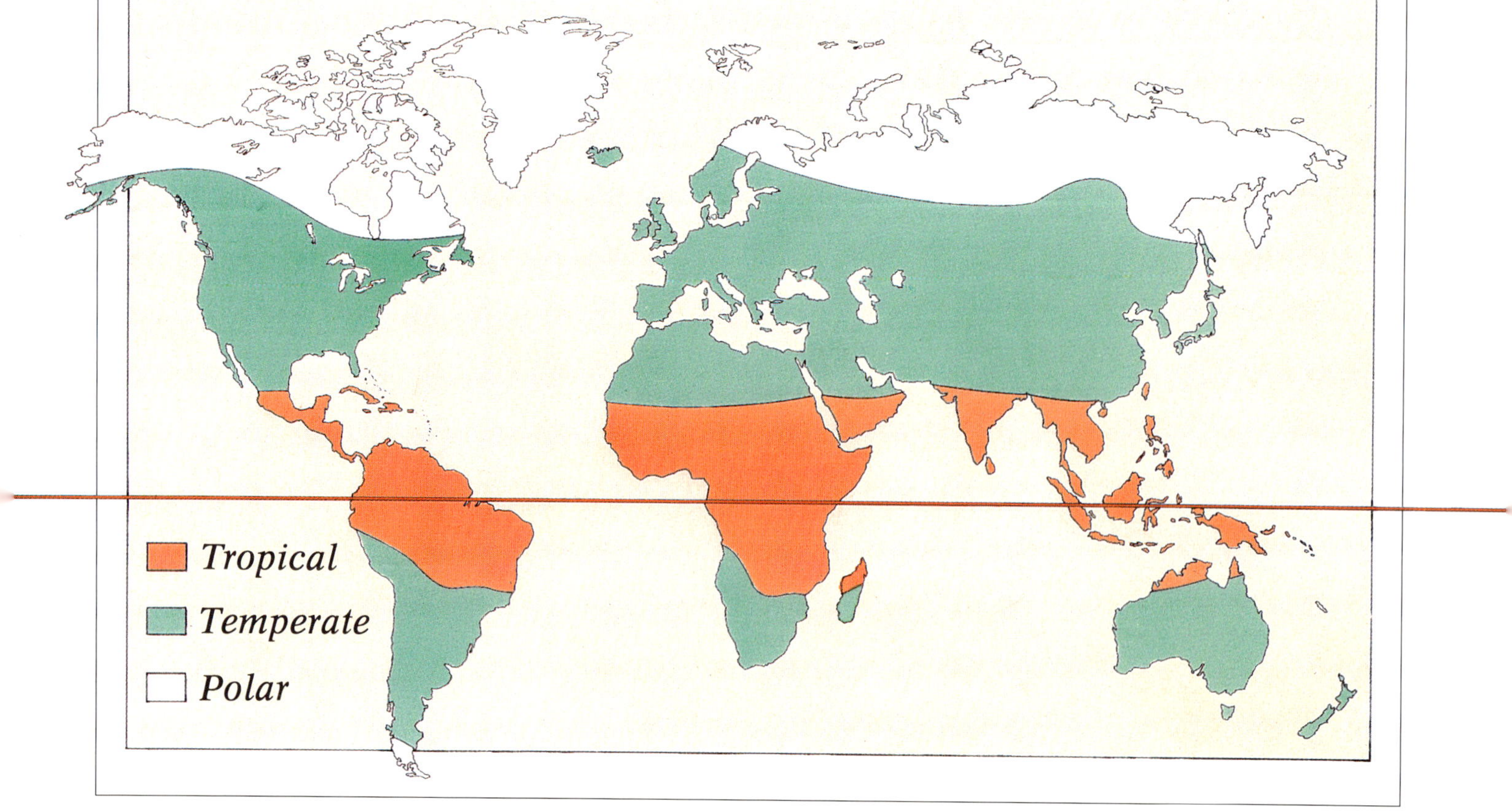

are ploughed and crops are planted. Many farm animals give birth to their young in spring.

Spring comes earlier to countries nearer the equator, for here the climate is warmer. By April southern California and southern Europe can be as warm as Holland or Ireland in midsummer. Where it is very hot, on and near the equator, there is no spring. There are only two seasons – a hot, wet one and a cooler, dry one – or it is hot and wet all year round.

Towards the poles, as it grows colder and colder, spring comes later. In the Arctic and Antarctic there is no spring and only a short summer. Even in summer temperatures are rarely over 10° C (50° F). Flowers do not appear in the Arctic until June and there are hardly any flowering plants in the Antarctic. Summer in the Antarctic is colder than most places in mid-winter.

'Spring' in the desert happens only when there is a rare fall of rain. Then, the desert looks like a carpet of flowers.

New leaves, new flowers

As spring sunshine warms the soil and spring rains moisten it, plants start to grow. Each tiny seed sends a rootlet down into the ground to gather nutrients and water. It also sends a shoot up through the soil into the air. This shoot produces leaves which use the energy in sunlight to make food from water, nutrients, and simple substances in the air. This food helps flowers to form.

A single flower may contain thousands of tiny pollen grains, the male parts of the plant, and a few much larger ovules, the female parts of the plant which contain unfertilized eggs. Wind or insects carry the pollen from flower to flower. Pollen reaching ovules fertilizes them and turns them into unripe seeds.

Many of the first spring flowers bloom on plants that had already made and stored their food the year before. Among these food stores are the kinds we know as bulbs. Bluebells, crocuses, daffodils, hyacinths, and tulips all grow from bulbs.

Spring garden flowers all come from ancestors found growing in the wild. Different regions have their own wild flowers that bloom in spring. North America is home to the colourful, delicate bloodroots, hepaticas, and spring beauties.

In northwest Europe, spring woods wear bright carpets of yellow primroses and celandines, pale pink wood anemones, and aptly named violets and bluebells. Most woodland spring flowers blossom before the leaves sprouting on the oaks or other trees above shut out the light.

Southern Europe's hillsides glow with colourful anemones, narcissi, irises, orchids, and tall asphodels. Here, and in southern California, some spring flowers reach their peak very early. Field poppy seeds sprout, flower and set ripe seeds before the short mild spring gives way to the hot, dry summer. Almond blossom tinges southern Spanish hillsides pink in January.

In Australia the native heaths are among the most common of spring flowers. Their flowering period extends well into summer.

The honey bee is the best known of the insects that pollinate flowers.

A seed contains a baby plant with a store of food which it uses to grow. After a seed has been buried in the soil it breaks open and sends out a tiny root to collect water and nutrients. Next it sends out a shoot that grows up through the soil and into the open air. On the shoot grow leaves which are used to gather energy from the sun.

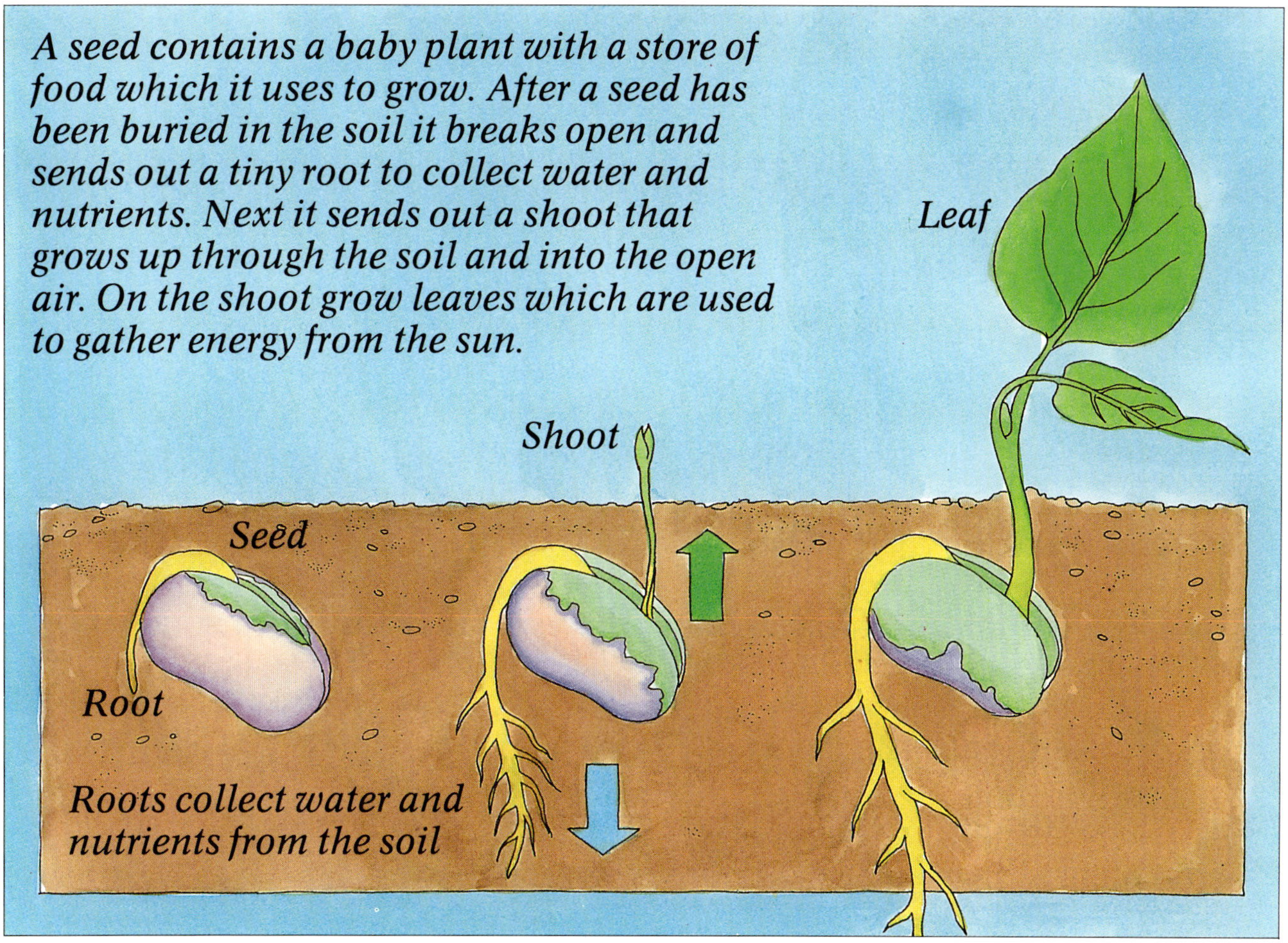

Snowdrops are among the earliest of spring flowers. As their name indicates they often come up when there is still snow on the ground.

Animals awakening

As spring sunshine warms the earth, creatures waken from their long winter rest.

Cold-blooded animals that have spent the winter fast asleep grow warm enough to move around. On sunny days, snakes and lizards creep out from holes and bask on sun-warmed leaves or logs. Frogs and freshwater turtles swim up from the muddy floors of ponds and lakes. Insect life begins to quicken. Ladybirds crawl out from under dead leaves littering woodland floors. Queen wasps start making paper nests from chewed-up wood. Butterflies that have survived the winter flit through sunlit meadows. Even on quite chilly days bumblebees buzz from flower to flower collecting pollen. Their dark colours soak up the sun's heat, while their 'furry' bodies trap enough of it to keep them active. Caterpillars that escaped the winter frost begin to move about in search of food. Many insects hatch from eggs their mothers laid the year before.

Warm-blooded beasts that have dozed away through winter wake up in spring. Bears leave their winter dens and dormice scramble from their nests among tree roots.

On mild nights, nocturnal animals appear. Slugs and beetles creep from cracks in soil or rotting logs. Some are snapped up by hedgehogs that leave winter nests of leaves and snuffle through the undergrowth. Newts, salamanders, and toads emerge from hiding places. High above, bats flutter from caves and lofts to hunt for moths.

After their long winter fast many creatures have grown thin and hungry. Eastern Europe's ground squirrels may have spent three-quarters of the year below ground and lost three-quarters of their weight. Some creatures do not survive hibernation. Eight out of ten hibernating dormice do not wake up in spring: they die of cold or hunger or have been eaten by predators while they slept.

Hedgehogs are one of the European animals that awake in spring.

In North America grizzly bears awake from their winter sleep in spring.

Winged migrants

Each April millions of swallows, warblers, shrikes, flycatchers, wagtails, and wading birds fly north from South America, Africa, or Australia to feed and breed in North America, Europe, and north Asia. In the southern spring the birds that have left the previous April for the northern spring return.

Some fly huge distances. Small songbirds called bobolinks fly up to 8000 km (5000 miles) north from Argentina. Like many migrant birds, bobolinks fly in flocks at night. Swallows are long-distance fliers too, and thousands wing their way from South Africa to northern Europe.

Most migrant birds fatten up before they make long, tiring journeys. On the way their bodies 'burn up' fat as fuel. Stored body fat gives even tiny hummingbirds the energy to cross large tracts of sea without a meal.

Surprisingly, big, powerful-looking storks, eagles, and buzzards choose the shortest way across a sea. For they are not strong fliers but soar or glide on air currents rising from warm land.

Each April birdwatchers glimpse thousands of the birds wheeling high across two narrow strips of sea where Europe almost touches Africa and Asia. In fact most migrant birds follow regular routes, called flyways. Scientists seek to identify these flyways by catching and ringing birds.

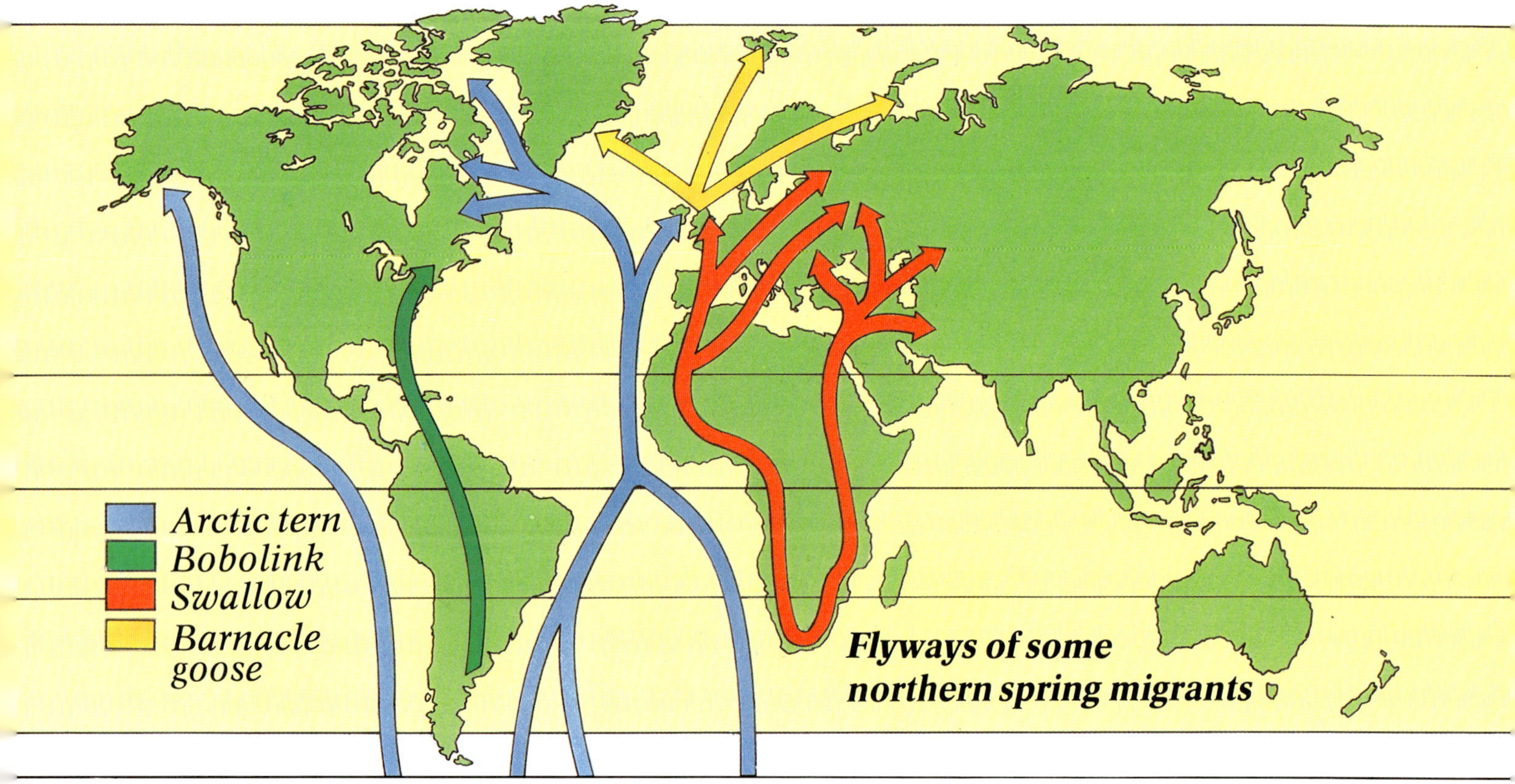

Flyways of some northern spring migrants

Barnacle geese migrate northwards to the Arctic in spring (see map below left).

As summer visitors reach Europe and North America, millions of other birds such as redwings, fieldfares, thrushes, ducks, geese and wading birds that wintered there head north to breed in northern forests or upon the boggy Arctic plains and coasts.

Birds are not the only winged migrants. Some butterflies and moths also migrate. One example is the Bogong moth which migrates from the low-lying land of south-eastern Australia up into the mountains in spring where it gathers in caves in very large numbers. The moths are very fat and the Aboriginals used to eat them as they were a good source of food.

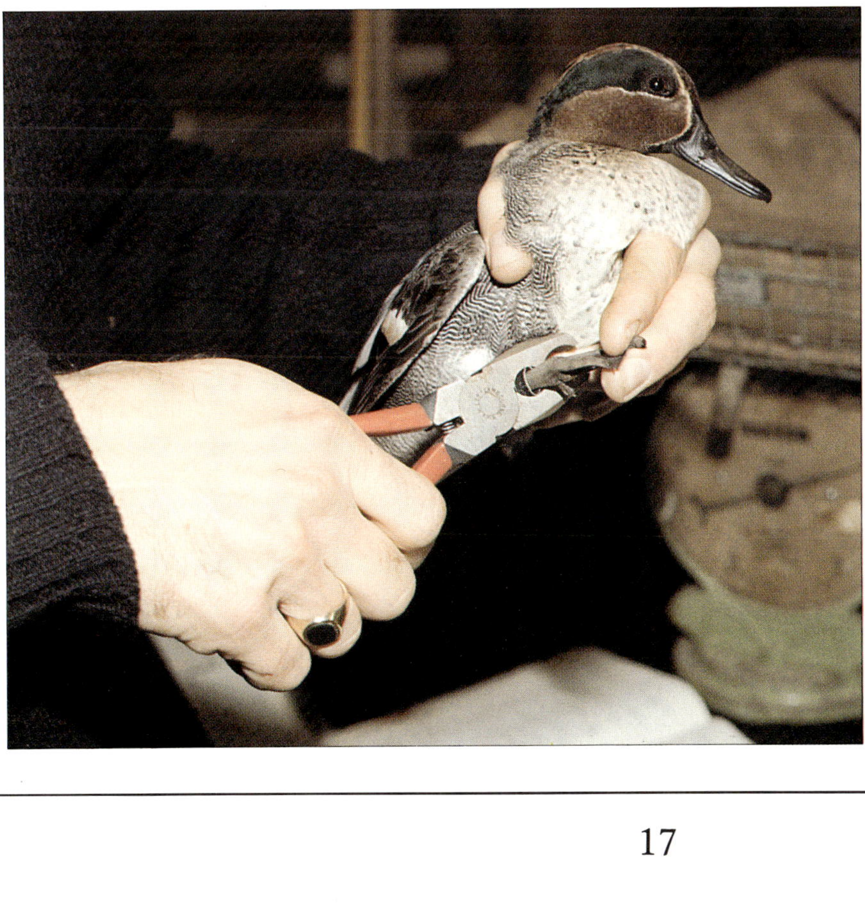

Ringing

One way to discover the flyways of migrating birds is ringing. A bird is caught in a special net and a metal ring, stating when and where the bird was captured, is put on the bird's leg. Each time the bird is recaptured the information on the ring is collected and the bird's movements can be traced. The bird (left) is being ringed.

New lives begin

Soon after migrant birds reach breeding grounds, each male claims a special patch of land and sings or shows off to scare rival males and win a female mate. Non-migrants like the European robin have already claimed a piece of woodland or garden and formed breeding pairs. Each pair of birds (sometimes only one) now builds a nest. In this the female lays her eggs, then sits on them for weeks to keep them warm until they hatch.

Meanwhile new life is also starting underground, in ponds and in the sea.

Badgers, foxes, rabbits, and some other mammals give birth to their young in burrows, many warmly lined with fur or leaves. The platypus, a special sort of mammal from Australia which lays eggs instead of bearing live young, also breeds in burrows during spring. Down there blind, naked babies start life in safety.

Breeding is also under way in ponds and sluggish streams. Soon after waking up from hibernation, male frogs and toads lie in the water croaking to attract a mate. When a female swims near, a male seizes her around the middle and fertilizes the eggs as she releases them. Male newts simply swim around the females

An egg contains a developing animal called an embryo which is attached to a food supply called a yolk. An embryo bird grows into a chick and when it fills the shell it uses a tiny tooth to break out of the shell.

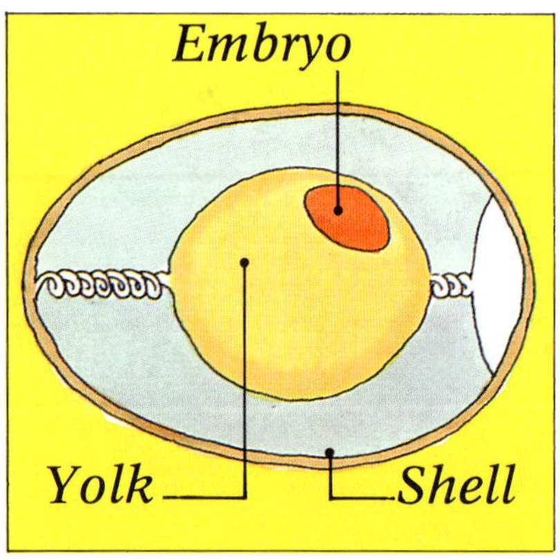

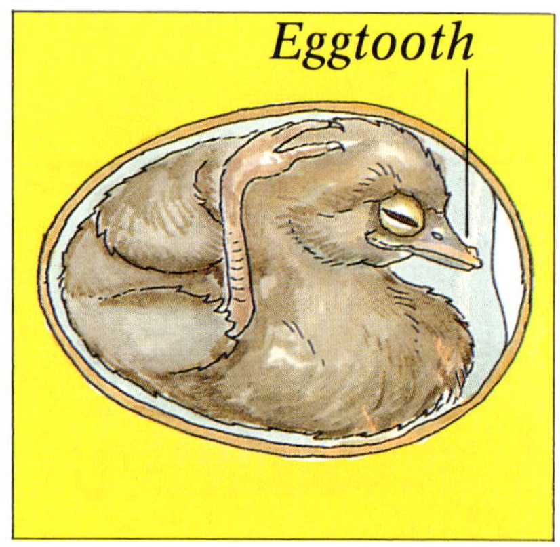

In spring fish called grunions swim on to Californian beaches to spawn.

waggling their showy tails and then deposit sperm which the female collects. Once paired, a female frog or toad lays many hundred of tiny eggs surrounded by clear jelly. Newts lay far fewer eggs and stick each to an underwater plant. After a few days, frog and toad eggs hatch into tiny legless tadpoles but newts have legs from the start.

In spring, freshwater fishes such as sticklebacks and carp lay their eggs, too. And in the sea, the strange horseshoe crabs and tiny fishes called grunions come ashore to spawn on sandy coasts of North America.

This bird called a dipper is fishing for food to feed its young.

Spring gardens

Gardens that had looked quite dead and bare all winter come alive with flowers in spring. First, crocuses produce their purple or yellow blooms. Then come the butter-coloured daffodils, with pansies, tulips, magnolias, and double-flowering cherries. After early blossoms wither, late spring flowers, such as clematis, laburnum and rhododendrons, begin to open.

In some European countries, where spring slowly takes the place of winter, spring flowers bloom for months. But in much of North America, spring is brief and quickly followed by hot summer sun. Here, spring flowers quickly fade and die.

The same spring flowers that brighten northern gardens in April or May also grow in mild climates of the Southern Hemisphere. But Australia's daffodils and double-flowering cherries are bursting into blossom in September, with the start of the southern spring.

Few gardeners just sit back and enjoy spring flowers. For spring is time to sow seeds, plant plants, and prune trees, to produce summer flowers, fruits, and vegetables.

In early spring, gardeners hoe dug ground to kill weed seedlings. They finish pruning fruit trees, and may cover these with nets to protect unopened buds from hungry birds.

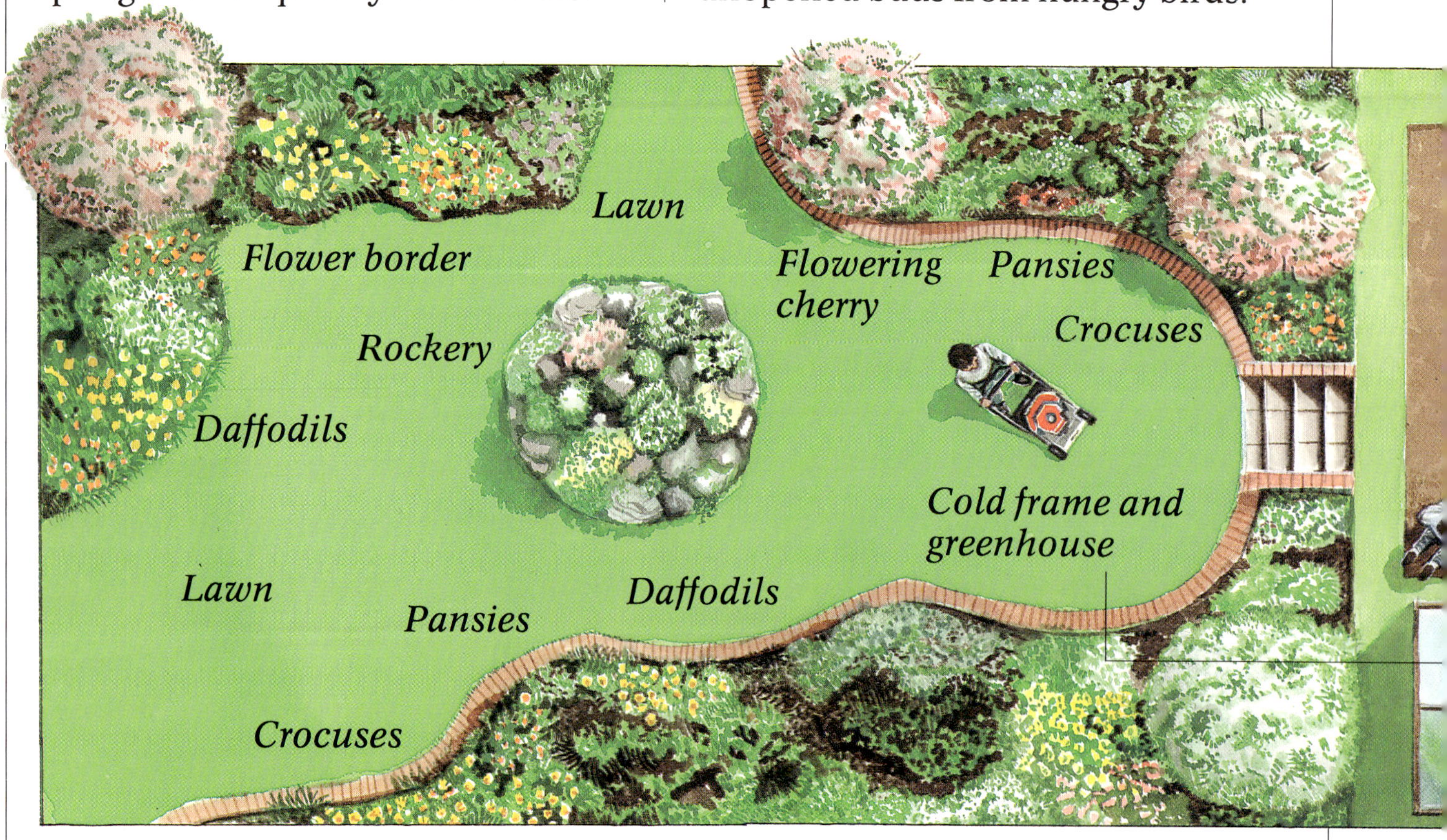

Spring is the time for planting seeds. This can be a family activity.

Lawn mowing starts when grass begins growing again.

If early spring is cold, gardeners may sow seeds of tomatoes, cabbages, marigolds and other plants in boxes kept indoors. Later, the young plants can be moved to a cold frame in the garden to 'harden off' before they are transplanted into open ground.

About the time that pear and peach trees bloom, gardeners begin sowing seed outdoors. Where frost is likely, they start with hardy plants like onions, lettuces, and marigolds. When apple blossom opens, and night frost ends, it should be safe to plant such tender crops as beans, maize, and most summer flowers.

Spring is a busy time for the gardener. Garden beds must be weeded and the soil dug over before the seeds of flowers and vegetables can be planted. As the weather warms the grass begins to grow and lawns must be mown. Tender young plants must be begun indoors or in a greenhouse. When planted out in the garden seedlings often need to be covered with nets to protect them from birds.

If the weather is cold, plants are often 'hardened off' in a cold frame before being planted in the garden.

Crop farming in spring

Spring is a busy time for farmers everywhere. Where frost and snow have melted, spring ploughing must be done. There may be farm manure or fertilizer to spread on the fields. Then farmers will sow seeds of many crops such as wheat or oats that ripen later in the year. On calm days farmers spray most crops to kill off weeds, pests and moulds. This can be done by hand, from a tractor, or from an aeroplane or helicopter.

There is work to do in orchards too. Fruit farmers finish pruning apple trees before these start to sprout. On cold nights they may burn old tyres or greenwood to trap warm air below the smoke and so stop frost killing tender blossoms.

As seeds begin to sprout in the fields of central North America and Europe, crops of southern regions of these continents are growing fast or are ready to be harvested. Spring is the time to prune grapevines and, by April, new leaves sprout from the dead-looking stumps all over southern Europe. Here, too, ripe oranges are hanging from the trees and broad beans are being picked. Spanish farmers are gathering potatoes. Greek olive growers collect ripe black olives fallen on the nets spread out beneath the olive trees.

In Australia, where the seasons are reversed, and winters are mild, wheat is already well grown when spring starts in September.

Ploughing
A typical scene in early spring is the farmer ploughing his field. This prepares the ground for planting. It breaks up the soil, covers the weeds and the remains of the last crop, and makes seedbeds.

Pruning vines

In spring it is time to prune the grape vines. If there are too many bunches of grapes on a vine, the quality of the fruit is not as good. Usually only four or five buds are left on a branch. Pruning is generally done by hand.

Crop spraying

In many parts of the world, crop spraying begins in spring. The land is sprayed to kill pests such as weeds and unwanted insects. Spraying is done by hand or from a tractor, aeroplane or even a helicopter.

Farm animals in spring

Spring is the time when many farm animals are born. Lambs, calves and foals are a common sight in the countryside. On cold Scottish hill farms, lambs are often born in the snow. Hill shepherds have to work hard taking the food from winter stores in the valleys up to the hungry sheep. In other parts of the world where it is not so cold, such as Australia, lambs are born much earlier.

On dairy farms, cows are grazing on lush new meadow grass and producing creamy milk. Spring is the time when a cow produces most milk. Many calves are born at this time too. On some farms calves are taken from their mothers and fed a milk substitute from buckets, so that there is more milk for the farmer to sell.

Many piglets are born in spring. Pigs give birth to large litters. There are sometimes as many as twelve piglets in a litter. Except for a few females who are kept to replace their mothers, the young pigs may be sold to another farmer who will fatten

In spring the Lapps go north with their reindeer herds.

them up for market. Young pigs are given lots of food so that they will grow quickly.

Hens produce more eggs in spring than at any other time of the year. Most hens are now kept in large sheds where their environment is controlled so that they produce as many eggs as possible all year round.

For certain shepherds, dairy farmers, and for reindeer herdsmen spring is time to travel. As snow melts on low slopes of the European Alps dairy farmers drive their cattle uphill from the valley floors. This is so their cows can graze on new grass in the mountain meadows. In the same way, shepherds drive their flocks from the lowlands where they spent the winter, to the uplands of the Pyrenees and other mountain ranges. Across Arctic Scandinavia and Russia, herdsmen called Lapps migrate with their half-wild reindeer. Herds of several thousand animals amble northward several hundred kilometres to summer breeding grounds on treeless Arctic plains.

Spring is lambing time in New Zealand.

Pre-Christian and Christian festivals

Some spring religious ceremonies have been celebrated for thousands of years. In olden days many people thought the sun was a god who died each winter and was born again next spring. In the short, dark days of winter food grew scarce, but as the sun regained its strength crops sprouted and farm animals were born. So each spring thankful people celebrated the rebirth of their god. Some called him Attis, others Adonis. North Europeans worshipped a mother goddess Eostre; from her name may come the word 'Easter'.

As the sun rose on the first day of spring, people danced and sang on hilltops. Then villagers walked in procession to an oak tree hung with evergreen mistletoe, a sign of everlasting life. Children gave each other eggs, a sign of life to come. Priests prayed for good crops. They killed lambs. Then the people feasted.

Christians changed this old pagan festival of Easter into a time of renewing faith in Jesus and God. The Christian Holy Week starts on Palm Sunday when people decorate churches with greenery in memory of the palm leaves thrown down to carpet Jesus' way into Jerusalem the week before he died. During Holy Week in the Spanish city of Seville there is a procession of huge floats that show scenes from the Bible story

At Whittle-le-Woods, England, a statue of the Virgin Mary is crowned on the first Monday in May.

During Holy Week in Seville men parade through the streets wearing hoods and cloaks.

of Easter. On Good Friday, Christians sadly remember the day that Jesus died. Many Mexicans even wear black for mourning. Then on Saturday at midnight, people light candles in churches to celebrate Jesus' coming alive again. In some countries they set off fireworks too. On Easter Day Christians sing hymns, give presents, and rejoice.

Forty days after Easter, Christians celebrate Ascension Day, the day when they believe Jesus finally rose to Heaven.

In northern lands, Easter and Ascension Day are both spring festivals. But in southern lands, they fall in autumn.

The Easter bunny was originally a hare who was a companion of the old goddess of spring, Eostre.

Jewish, Hindu, Sikh and Buddhist festivals

Spring is an important time of the year for many faiths. Each March or April, Jewish families celebrate Pesach (Passover). This marks the spring grain harvest in Palestine. It also remembers the time when the Jews were enslaved in Egypt and how important it was that they held together to free themselves from slavery.

The first and main Passover event is Seder night. Each family reads how its ancestors hastily prepared to leave Egypt. Like them, the family eats a special meal. There is bread made without yeast. The family shares bitter herbs as reminders of the bitter times their ancestors endured in Egypt. Fresh lettuce stands for spring. Wine stands for freedom and joy. Then comes a fruit-nut-and-wine mixture called *charoset* that looks like clay. This recalls the cities built by Jews in Egypt.

In March or April Hindus everywhere enjoy the lively Hindu festival of *Holi*. This marks the spring wheat harvest and celebrates an old legend about a prince who escaped from the wicked goddess Holika. People light bonfires, and streak their foreheads with bonfire ash for luck. They play outdoor games and lively pranks, throwing coloured water and

Above *This family has gathered at the Seder table to celebrate the beginning of the Pesach (Passover).*

Right *This beautiful stained-glass window of the Seder table is in the Central Synagogue in London.*

This is an offering for Ch'ing Ming, *Hong Kong.*

red powder at anyone who passes. Sikhs have a similar festival, called *Hola Mohallah.* On 13 April, Sikhs and Hindus both celebrate their New Year's Day. For Sikhs and Hindus in the Southern Hemisphere these festivals occur in autumn.

Chinese, Japanese and other Asian peoples also celebrate in March or April. *Ch'ing Ming* (Pure Brightness) is a Chinese spring festival when members of each family get together. People sweep their ancestors' graves, eat special meals, and rekindle hearth fires. On 8 April, Japanese Buddhists enjoy a colourful flower festival in honour of the Buddha's birthday.

These people are celebrating the Hindu festival of Holi.

Special spring days

Here are some holidays and other special days that fall in spring in most parts of the world.

Children and grown-ups often play tricks on each other on 1 April: April Fools' Day. The victims are called April fools in England and America, but April fish in France. Some say the first April fools were people who went on celebrating New Year's Day on 1 April after a new calendar shifted it to 1 January in 1564; but April foolery goes back to ancient times.

Arbor Day – a day for planting trees – occurs in April in most northern states of the USA. The English mark 23 April as St George's Day in honour of their patron saint.

May Day has been a special day for many hundreds of years. In the old days English villagers used to dance around a maypole and crown a May queen, and morris dancers performed. Most of this goes back to ancient festivals. In the USA some children make a paper May basket, fill it with flowers and sweets, and hang it on a friend's door. American families honour their mothers on Mother's Day, the second Sunday in May, and on Memorial Day, at the end of the month they remember American soldiers killed in war. In Britain and some other countries Mother's Day is celebrated in March.

North of the equator these events take place in spring. South of the equator they happen in late summer or autumn.

The southern spring is the time of the year when many agricultural shows are held in Australia and many places give school children a special holiday so they may go to the show in the capital city of their state. In New Zealand as well as Australia Guy Fawkes Day or Bonfire Night as it is sometimes called is a spring celebration. On the night of November 5 there are big fireworks displays, remembering when Guy Fawkes tried to blow up the English Parliament.

Dancing around a maypole is a traditional May Day celebration in England.

On Memorial Day in the USA there are parades to honour soldiers.

Games, sports and recreations

Spring is when some of the best known children's games begin. Tag and skipping are two games that children mostly start to play in spring. In the catching game of tag, one boy or girl is 'it' and chases all the rest. Those caught are 'tagged' unless already touching wood. Some spring skipping games go back to ancient times when people jumped or swung on swings to make the crops grow high.

At Easter many people play games with Easter eggs. On Easter Day European children may search their homes for chocolate eggs hidden by their parents. Greeks bang red eggs together: the last to crack is said to bring its owner luck. In parts of Europe and America children roll Easter eggs down slopes in races.

Easter parades are also spring events in northern lands. In Atlantic City, for example, people dress up and parade through streets. The best-dressed person wins a prize. Many fairs and agricultural shows are also spring events, some of which include parades where people wear traditional costumes or fancy dress, or lead prize animals.

For centuries, Easter Monday has been a time for ball games such as handball, football, skittles, and stoolball. Now, thousands of families watch sports like horse racing and

Morris dancing is a popular spring recreation in Britain.

Many fairs and parades are held in spring, such as this one in Seville in Spain.

motor racing on that special holiday.

Several world famous sports events take place in spring. For instance, England's Oxford and Cambridge Boat Race and the Grand National Steeplechase occur in late March or early April. In the United States, the Kentucky Derby horse race is run on the first Saturday in May. The Melbourne Cup, Australia's foremost horse race, is run in the southern spring month of November.

Lastly, summer sports like baseball, cricket, and lawn tennis start in spring. England's cricket season starts in April, when it is autumn in Australia. Down under, test matches begin about November.

The Kentucky Derby is one of the famous horse races run in spring.

Spring in art and literature

Poets, novelists, and naturalists have written about the changing countryside in spring. Here is just a taste of their impressions.

The English poetess Sara Coleridge (1802-1852) noticed how each spring month brought something new:

March brings breezes, loud and shrill,
Stirs the dancing daffodil.

April brings the primrose sweet,
Scatters daisies at our feet.

May brings flocks of pretty lambs.
Skipping by their fleecy dams.

Above *Detail of 'Primavera' ('Spring') by Sandro Botticelli (1440-1510).*

The novelist D.H. Lawrence found that spring came very early in the year in northern Italy:

Spring starts in February, with the winter aconite . . . The clenched little nuggets of the aconite puff out, they become light bubbles, like small balloons, on a green base.

In Argentina, a Southern Hemisphere country, spring comes at the opposite time of year, as the naturalist W.H. Hudson reminds us:

When, in July and August, I watched for the coming spring, it was the migrants, the birds that came annually to us from the far north, that chiefly attracted me . . . The most striking of the newcomers was the small scarlet tyrant-bird . . . all shining scarlet except the black wings and tail.

Spring scenes appear in countless paintings. Perhaps the most famous of all is 'Primavera' ('Spring') by the Italian artist Sandro Botticelli (1444-1510). This shows the love goddess Venus in a flowery meadow, with a maiden representing spring.

Opposite *Detail of a painting by Jean Fragonard (1732-1806) called 'Spring'.*

Spring sayings, songs, and rhymes

Spring sayings, songs, and rhymes in English are mostly about the weather of the northern spring. Not all sayings prove true but they give an idea of the weather likely in each month.

'March comes in like a lion and goes out like a lamb,' means that fierce winds often blow in early March, but the end of the month can be mild. 'A peck of March dust is worth a king's ransom,' means that dry weather in early spring dries the soil enough for sowing seeds.

If April starts rough and blustery some people say, 'April borrowed from March three days, and they were ill.'

In old rhymes and sayings, May is the favourite month. A verse from one old ballad says:

There are twelve months in all the year,
As I hear many men say,
But the merriest month in all the year
Is the merry month of May.

Another rhyme remembers an old May superstition:

That fair maid who, at break of day,
Goes to the fields on the first of May,
And washes in dew from the hawthorn tree
Shall ever afterwards beautiful be.

The dew of May morning was also thought to be a cure for many diseases such as gout, goitre and consumption.

One rhyme is about the bees in May:

A swarm of bees in May is worth a load of hay;
A swarm of bees in June is worth a silver spoon;
A swarm of bees in July is hardly worth a fly.

This means that an early swarm has all summer to collect nectar and pollen to make honey, but a late swarm may not have time to collect sufficient to make enough honey to feed itself all winter.

As late as May spring weather can be chancy. One proverb warns:

Cast ne'er a clout
Till May be out.

This might mean you should wear warm clothes until the end of May, or until hawthorn (May) blossom appears. A reminder that even late spring mornings can be chilly comes in this well-known children's song:

Here we come gathering nuts in May,
Nuts in May, nuts in May,
Here we come gathering nuts in May
On a cold, and frosty morning.

Now is the month of maying

Now is the month of maying
When merry lads are playing, fa la
Each with his bonny lass
Up on the greeny grass, fa la

The Spring, clad all in gladness,
Doth laugh at Winter's sadness, fa la
And to the bagpipe's sound
The nymphs tread out their ground.
Fa la.

Fie then! why sit we musing
Youth's sweet delight refusing? fa la
Say, dainty nymphs, and speak,
Shall we play barley-break? Fa la.

by Thomas Morley

The beauty of spring has inspired many songwriters.

Things to do with nature

Here are some things to do to help you study plants and animals in spring. Soak some bird seed. Then plant it in a bowl of moist soil indoors. After a few days you should see seedlings pushing shoots above the soil. You might also grow watercress seeds on damp blotting paper in a foil dish. Sprinkle the seeds onto damp blotting paper you have placed in a little water in a foil dish. Keep the dish in a dark place until the sprouts are 4 cm (1.6 in) high then place it in the light. The blotting paper must be kept damp.

Stick a twig with buds on in water. Examine the buds day by day. Watch them open and produce new leaves. To take a look inside a large bud simply cut open a tightly closed cabbage.

A tree's growing buds take nourishment from sap that rises inside the tree trunk. In parts of Canada and the USA people collect the sugary sap of sugar maples. Then they boil the sap to make maple syrup.

Growing watercress in a foil dish

Foil dish Blotting paper Water

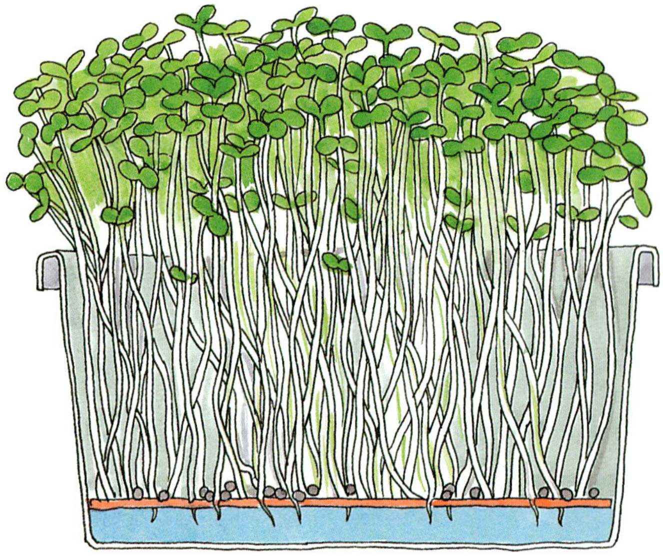

Many spring flowers grow from bulbs. To find out how a bulb is made slice an onion down through the middle. Notice its many layers. Each layer is a thick leaf full of stored food.

A cut cabbage

Twig with buds and leaves in water

Keeping a field diary

Some spring flowers bloom much earlier than others. Keep a flower diary, and write down when each kind first appears. A flower field guide could help you recognize the different species. Notice which insects pollinate which flowers.

You could also use your diary to write down when different birds first start singing. (Some start in winter.)

Notice how garden birds behave to one another in spring. Watch parents building nests, but take care not to disturb the nests or eggs, or frighten the parents away.

Peer closely in a pond and count the kinds of tiny creatures living there. Some of you might make a garden pond for frogs. Simply dig a large hole and waterproof it with a pond liner. Then fill with water. Add some frog spawn and see how it develops into tadpoles. Tadpoles can also be kept in large jars.

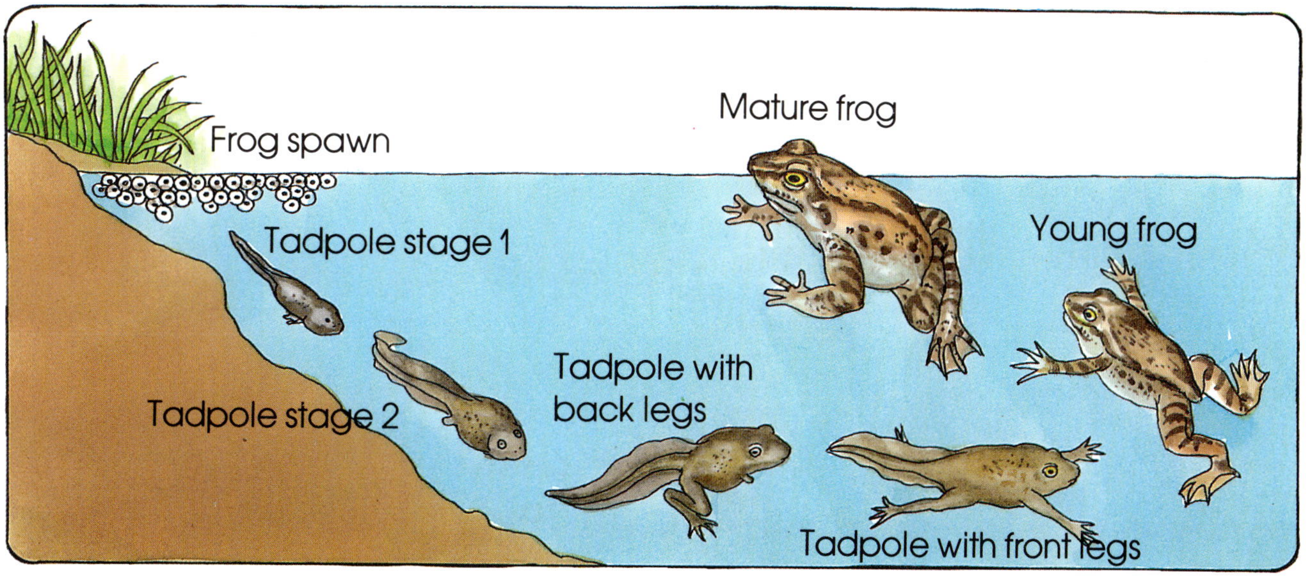

Things to do with food

Here are some ways of making or decorating foods for spring festivities. **Ask an adult to help before you begin.**

Decorating eggs
To colour an Easter egg red, boil it with a beetroot. If you boil it with onion skin it will turn gold, and spinach makes it green. Or, with a wax crayon, draw a pattern on a boiled egg, then dip it in dye. The dye colours all except the wax pattern. You can also decorate a hard-boiled egg by painting on a face, then adding bits of coloured wool for hair and perhaps a beard.

Draw on egg with wax crayon

Decorate egg

Easter cakes Take 230 g (8 oz) of self-raising flour, 110 g (4 oz) of margarine, a pinch of salt, half a teaspoon of allspice, an egg, and 60 g (2 oz) of currants. Beat the margarine and sugar until creamy. Sift the flour, salt, and spice. Then beat spoonfuls of them into the creamy mixture alternately with spoonfuls of beaten egg. Add the currants. Roll out the mixture and cut out biscuit shapes. Prick these with a fork. Place them on a greased baking sheet and bake at 180° C (350° F) for 20 minutes.

Charoset

You might also make *charoset*, one of the foods eaten at the Jewish Seder meal. Take 230 g (8 oz) of apples, 60 g (2 oz) of raisins, 60 g (2 oz) of almonds or walnuts, some cinnamon, and a little sweet wine. Peel and core the apples, and chop them with the nuts and raisins. Add enough cinnamon to taste, then add the wine. Mix all into a tasty paste.

More things to do

Making a windvane

Spring weather can be windy, so make a windvane to find wind direction. Draw a broad arrow on cardboard, then cut it out. Now stick a large needle or a hat pin from edge to edge through the middle of the arrow. Then stick the end of the pin into an eraser. Make sure the arrow turns freely around its pin. Take the windvane outside and hold it up in the wind by the eraser. The arrow should turn and point into the wind.

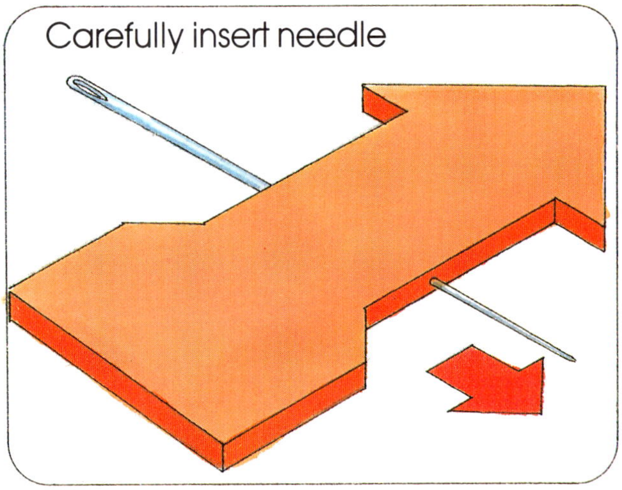

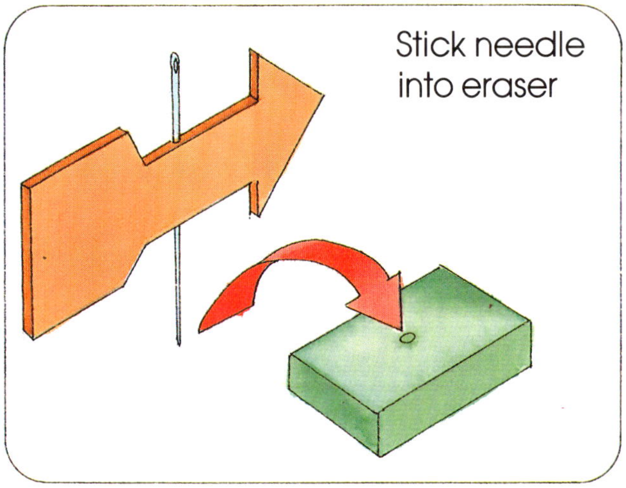

Hunters and Hares

Outdoor tracking games are fun for groups of people. Two act as hares, the rest as hunters. Ten minutes after the hares set off, the hunters try to find them. They follow clues the hares have left behind. In towns chalk arrows mean 'this way' crosses mean 'not this way'. An arrow pointing from a '5' inside a square means 'message hidden five paces away'. A dot in a circle means 'gone home'. In the country, hares use sticks or stones to make clues instead of chalk marks.

Making a kite

Make notches in both ends of a long and a short stick. The sticks must be thin, light and strong. Lay the short stick across the long stick above its middle. Lash both together with thin string. Tie another string to the end of one of the sticks and then stretch it around the frame, through the notches, then tie again. Cover the frame with a piece of paper, polythene, or thin fabric and cut to fit. Fasten it to the frame with some sticky tape. Now tie one slack string to one end of each stick and pass both strings loosely through a curtain ring before tying them to the opposite ends of the sticks. Tie a towing line to the ring. Lastly, make a long tail for your kite. Use string with paper strips tied to it.

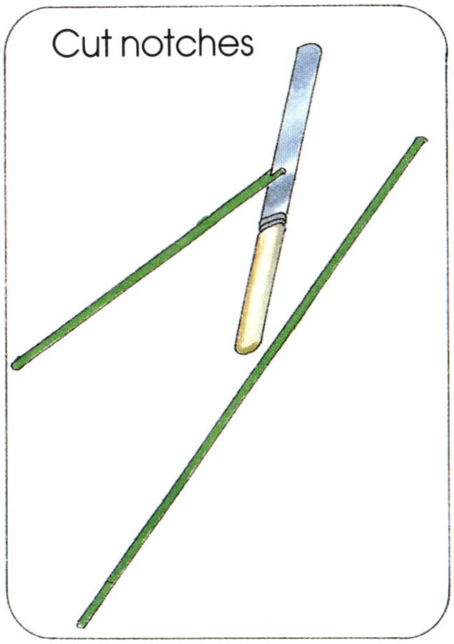

Cut notches

Lash sticks together

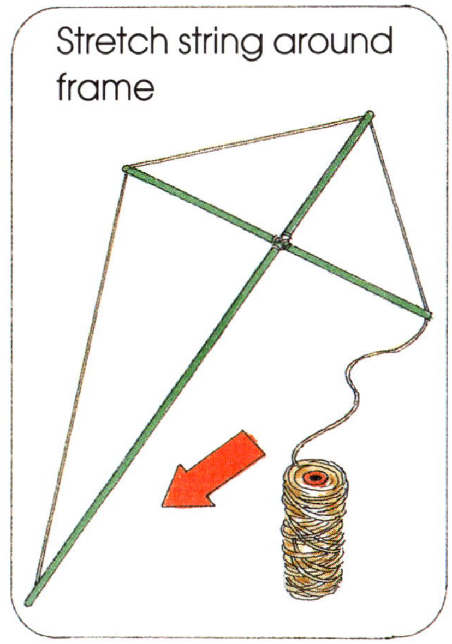

Stretch string around frame

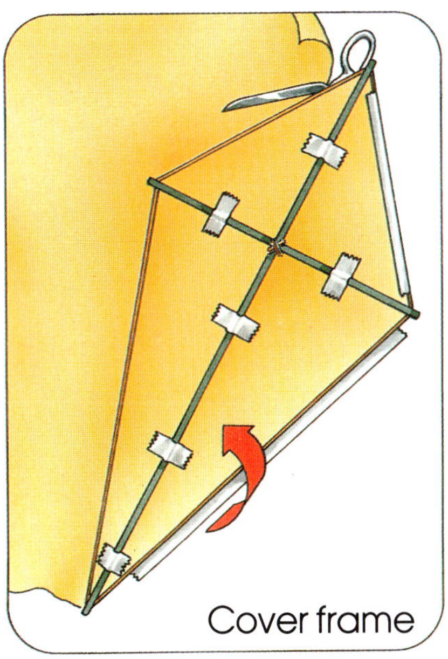

Cover frame

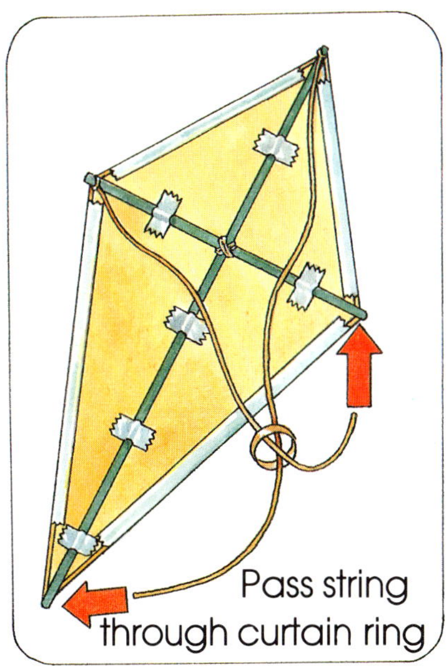

Pass string through curtain ring

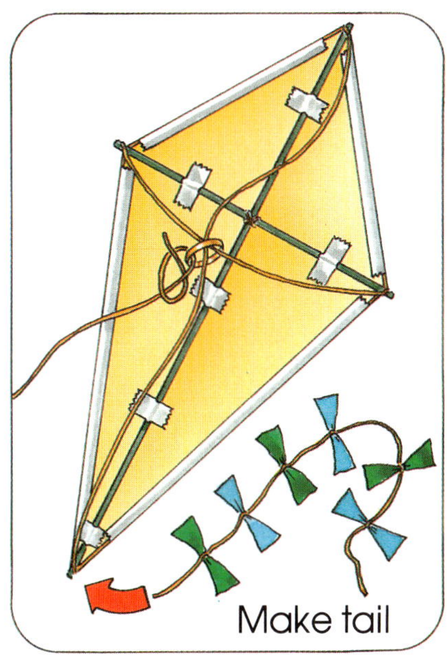

Make tail

Glossary

April Fools' Day The first day of April, when people play jokes on one another.
Arbor Day A day in early spring when people plant trees in the USA. Arbor Day falls on different dates in different states.
Bulb Mass of tightly packed leaves and buds that store food for making flowers like daffodils or hyacinths.
Ch'ing Ming **(Pure Brightness)** Family spring festival celebrated by the Chinese.
Easter An old spring festival, and the religious festival in March or April when Christians mourn Jesus' death and celebrate his coming alive again.
Equinox A period which occurs twice a year when day and night are of equal length. One equinox marks the beginning of spring; the other equinox marks the beginning of autumn.
Fast A period when people deliberately don't eat, usually as part of a religious celebration.
Hola Mohallah A spring festival celebrated by Sikhs.
Holi Hindu spring festival when people throw coloured water and red powder at each other.
Lapps Nomadic reindeer herdsmen of far northern Europe.
May Day The first of May, once set aside for spring festivities. Communist countries such as the USSR hold huge May Day parades.
Migrants Animals that make long journeys to reach feeding or breeding grounds. Each spring some migrant birds fly almost half way around the world.
Morris dance A traditional English folk dance.
Orbit The path of the earth around the sun, or the path of a body in space around another body in space.
Pesach (Passover) Jewish spring festival that celebrates, among other things, the Jews' escape from Egypt long ago.
Sap Watery juice in plants. In spring sap rises in tree trunks and helps new leaves to grow.
Seder A ceremonial meal eaten on the first night of the Jewish festival of Pesach (Passover).
Solstice Either the longest or the shortest day of the year. The longest day of the year marks the beginning of summer and the shortest day of the year marks the beginning of winter.
Spawn To mate and deposit eggs, to breed.
Sperm A male cell which can enter an egg cell and fertilize it. From this fertilized egg a new organism grows.
Temperate A region having a mild climate, intermediate between a cold polar climate and hot tropical climate. Most temperate areas are in the middle latitudes (see map on page 10).
Tornadoes Whirling funnels of air that form where warm and cold air meet. Each spring many tornadoes occur in the southern USA and in the USSR.

Further reading

Burton, Jane, **The Book of the Year** (Frederick Warne, 1983).
Fox, Julian, **Easter** (Wayland, 1984).
Gerrard, Peter A., **Nature through the Seasons** (Midas Books, 1976).
Goaman, Muriel, **Your Book of the Year** (Faber and Faber, 1963).
Kapoor, Dr Sukhbir Singh, **Sikh Festivals** (Wayland, 1985).
Maclean, Colin and Moira, **A Book of Spring** (Studio Vista/Cassell Collier Macmillan, 1975).
Mitter, Swasti, **Hindu Festivals** (Wayland, 1985).
Reeves, James, **The Springtime Book** (William Heinemann, 1976).
Turner, Reuben, **Jewish Festivals** (Wayland, 1985).
Vaughan, Jenny, **The Easter Book** (Macdonald Educational, 1980).
Woodward, John and Luff, Peter **The Field Guide: A Farmland Companion** (Blandford Press, 1983).

Picture acknowledgements

The publishers would like to thank the following for allowing their photographs to be reproduced in this book: Bridgeman Art Library 34, 35; Bruce Coleman Ltd 12 (Freider Sauer), 19 (above/Jeff Foott, below/E. Breeze-Jones), 32 (Colin Molyneux); Cephas Picture Library 5 (Mick Rock), 8 (Mick Rock), 26 (Frank B. Higham), 30 (D. Burrows); Geoscience Features Picture Library 11, 13, 31; Hutchison Library 25 (R. Ian Lloyd), 27 (Liba Taylor), 29 (above/Lesley Nelson, below/Tim Beddaw); Photri 9 (below), 27 (below/A. Novak), 33 (below); Royal Society for the Protection of Birds 16 (above/C.H. Gommersall); Sonya Halliday Photographs 28 (right); Tony Stone Worldwide *cover*; Wildfowl Trust, Slimbridge 17 (below/J.B. Blossom), ZEFA Picture Library 4 (W.H. Mueller), 7 (Photri), 9 (above/Golebiowski), 14 (H. Reinhard), 21 (above/Teasey, below/Corneel Voigt), 24 (W. Schmidt), 28 (left/Neville Kenton), 33 (above/Haro Schumacher). All artwork is by the Hayward Art Group.

Index